THE LOONY DOG O HANDBOO

Borin Van Loon

CENTURY PUBLISHING

LONDON

To the Loony Dog-owner

(A note from the author)
To all of you who have already read
exhaustively and watched extensively other
well-known books and television series on dogs
by other renowned doggy experts and who have
already expended vast reserves of physical and
nervous energy on the more conventional
attempts to obtain the co-operation of Man's
Best Friend (sic) in the ordinary decencies of
everyday existence, to you who, despite your
best endeavours, have finally, at the end of your
moral and financial reserves, and having
become a closet Special Brew (or equivalent
beverage) addict in order to cope with strain
and social embarrassment caused by your
animal, decided that your dog is – simply put –
a perfect bastard, the present volume is
dedicated.

The Dog

Quiescence

Dogs spend virtually all their time in
Contemplative Introspection* (read this again
slowly, it's one of the few 'plusses' in the whole
book).

* When not engaged in the throughput of liquids and
  solids (see 'Feeding' and 'Toiletting').

Common Positions

side elevation

end elevation

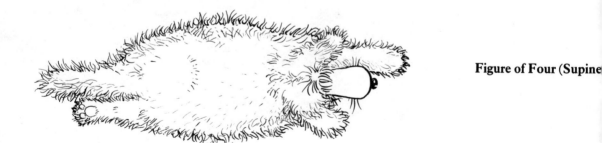

plan

Figure of Four (Supine)

Figure of Four (Standing)

Common Positions

The Kneel

The Ultra-kneel (or Foetal)
Notable for proximity of sensitive
nose to anal aperture (see 'Methane
Output')

Common Positions

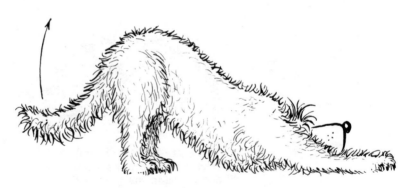

(Seen From Rear)

Salaam (Forward Stretch)

Often followed by Reach (Rear Stretch)

Particularly prevalent following periods of repose.

Common Positions

Tripod

Failed Tripod

Cutaway Diagrams
Showing most important features of each animal.

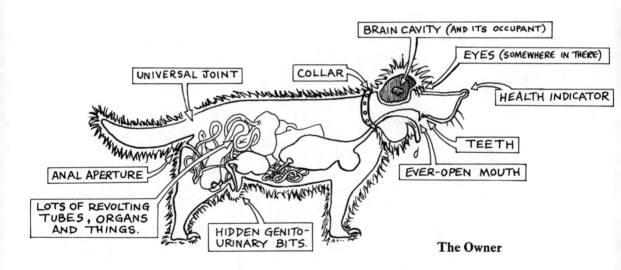

UNIVERSAL JOINT

COLLAR

BRAIN CAVITY (AND ITS OCCUPANT)

EYES (SOMEWHERE IN THERE)

HEALTH INDICATOR

TEETH

EVER-OPEN MOUTH

ANAL APERTURE

LOTS OF REVOLTING TUBES, ORGANS AND THINGS.

HIDDEN GENITO-URINARY BITS.

The Owner

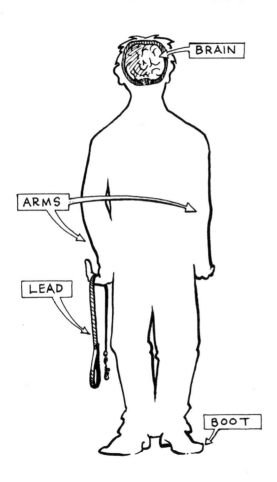

The Owned

It will be noted that the brain at right is much larger than the brain at left. If this is the case, how is it that both subjects often act equally stupidly, e.g. how does the one with the larger brain become a loony dog-owner in the first place? (This in no way reflects upon those with the intelligence to purchase this book.)

Exercising the Dog and Your Nerves

Other books may tell you that a healthy, happy dog needs at least an hour's exercise every day, preferably off the lead, playing with a ball in a field or park, whatever the weather. The poor loony dog-owner who actually believes any of this will rapidly learn differently when trying to put such advice into practice. . . .

. . . What the books might further mention is that exercising your dog will only be a pleasure if you have managed to instil in him the rudiments of discipline through training. To the loony dog-owner this is clearly laughable and sadly ironic.

Walking the Dog (off the lead)

Absence Makes The Voice Grow Louder

Walking the Dog (off the lead)

Early attempts to follow expert advice about letting the dog run free will usually be disastrous and deter the loony dog-owner from ever trying it again. This is because even in the most remote countryside there is no guarantee that another dog – or something vaguely resembling it – will not appear over the horizon.

Never underestimate your dog's powers of distant observation (despite his apparent inability to find a choc-drop lying on the floor in front of him without sniffing it out) as he will invariably disappear in the direction of the distraction never (one might be tempted to hope) to be seen again.

What is so terrible about the loony dog, when off the lead, meeting another dog? Well, the mental age of such an animal being seldom more than two months, it therefore has never developed the social niceties whereby a quick wag and a sniff does not develop into all-out combat. This is bad news. (See 'Social Skills')

The only really safe place to exercise the loony dog off the lead would be the middle of the Sahara desert. . . .

The loony dog-owner will soon decide that other methods of exercise must be found unless, that is, he is totally irresponsible and continues to inflict himself and his dog on the rest of the world (such people do exist).

Walking the Dog (on the lead)

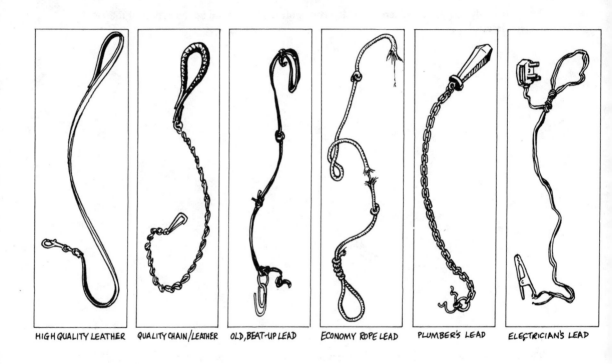

HIGH QUALITY LEATHER   QUALITY CHAIN/LEATHER   OLD, BEAT-UP LEAD   ECONOMY ROPE LEAD   PLUMBER'S LEAD   ELECTRICIAN'S LEAD

Types of Lead

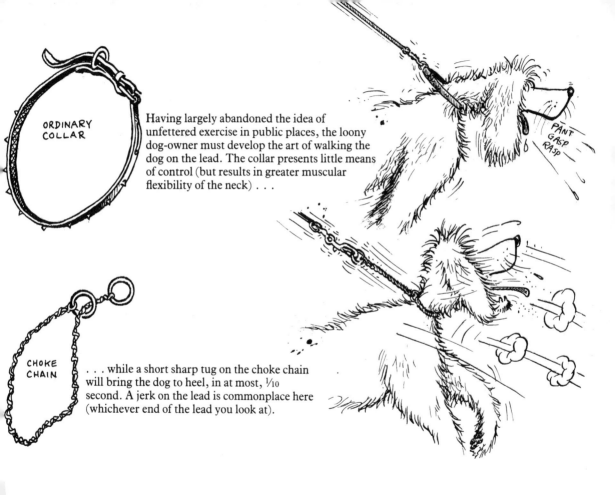

ORDINARY COLLAR

Having largely abandoned the idea of unfettered exercise in public places, the loony dog-owner must develop the art of walking the dog on the lead. The collar presents little means of control (but results in greater muscular flexibility of the neck) . . .

PANT GASP RASP

CHOKE CHAIN

. . . while a short sharp tug on the choke chain will bring the dog to heel, in at most, $\frac{1}{10}$ second. A jerk on the lead is commonplace here (whichever end of the lead you look at).

Walking the Owner (on the lead)

Novice loony dog-owners may be tempted to adopt the Nonchalant Lean at a 45° angle to the onward thrust of movement, however one of the first features of loony dog forward progress to be learnt . . .

. . . is its volatility: a series of random jerks rather than a smooth onward pull. These are instantaneous responses to ever-changing aural, nasal and visual stimuli (see 'Bloody Nuisances').

Walking the Dog (on the lead)

The one quality required by the loony dog-owner –
apart, that is, from consummate stupidity – is having
constant 360° vision. In other words having eyes in the
back of the head.

The idea is to spot potential instinctual canine triggers (or 'Bloody Nuisances') before the dog does. Here are some:

Walking the Dog (on the lead)

Never be caught unawares like this poor fool whose psychopathic animal has just spotted the items on the page before last.

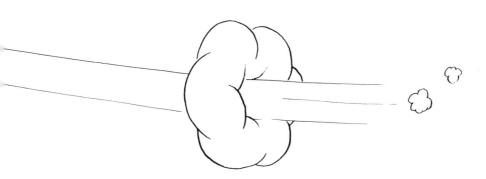

Grappling Skills

Various gambits can be employed by the ingenious loony dog-owner in the avoidance of Bloody Nuisances (either real or potential), but a vital prerequisite is the acquisition of 'Grappling Skills'. In extremity the Close Embrace might be employed. This does have the advantage of temporarily immobilising the animal in the throes of its hysteria (yelps, screams, barking, supercanine thrashing, scrabbling, powerful jolts on the lead, etc.) and does force his eyes away from the trigger but can result in aching forearms and might increase the blood pressure of the loony dog-owner. Not recommended in public places.

The Close Embrace

Grappling Skills

A much more effective treatment of the problem is to intercept the rays of light from the instinctual trigger in question (which is the indirect cause of the uproar) as they travel in a straight line towards the canine retinas and optic nerves. In other words: clapping your hand over the dog's eyes. This is very effective, particularly if you can manage to spot the instinctual trigger before the dog does and prevent his (un)predictable response.

Of course, even the dimmest animal will eventually twig that there is something out there that he should be seeing/meeting/having a go at (particularly if he can also smell or hear an oncoming trigger – jingling collars and leads have a lot to answer for). A pre-emptive measure is to grab the scruff of the neck with the other hand to arrest any spasmodic wriggles or jerks of the head in its attempt to peep.

The Hoodwink

Grappling Skills

Many other methods of physical restraint can be deployed experimentally in combination with jerks on the lead, but it will often be found that the true loony dog – once triggered – possesses the kick of a donkey and the wriggling power of a Houdini. Never underestimate his powers of escapology both from your arms and from his collar. Many a loony dog-owner has learnt the hard way that over-enthusiasm in grappling has resulted in an equal and opposite reaction and the dog has escaped.

Avoidance Tactics (in the park)

Avoidance Tactics (in the park)

Working with an Accomplice

Finding the Gap

Avoidance Tactics
(in the country)

Out of the Frying Pan . . .

Avoidance Tactics (on the beach)

Walking the Dog (on the rope)

Having discarded any idea of letting the dog off the lead, the loony dog-owner may experience an insidious feeling of guilt that the animal is not getting enough exercise. The evidence for this will be frantic muscular spasms where the dog charges about clawing large portions of pile out of the carpet and knocking furniture and people for six.

This is a dubious means of exercising.

A length of rope connecting the lead and the choke chain theoretically solves the problem. It means the dog can't run off but can stretch his legs, can be wound in by the loony dog-owner at the approach of other dogs – followed by an appropriate avoidance strategy – and can be paid out again to enable relatively free running. . . .

It's actually more like trying to fly a five-hundredweight kite in a tornado, blindfold.

Walking the Dog (on the rope)

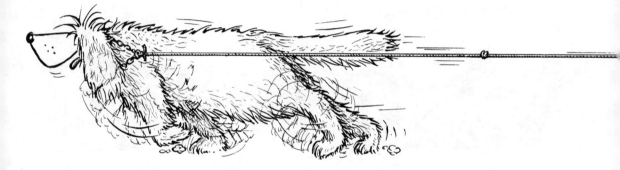

The Water Skier
(can result in new pair of shoes)

Walking the Dog (on the rope)

Bobbing and Weaving (can result in dizzy spells)

Rounding up a Stranger (can result in dislocated jaw and black eye)

Walking the Dog (on the rope)

After some use of this technique the loony dog-owner will notice tight knots appearing in the rope – no matter how fastidious he is. These knots, combined with the deleterious effects of dirt, moisture, urine (the rope inevitably interposes into the line of fire during cocking-of-the-leg situations) eventually become weak points, liable to snap under sudden strain.

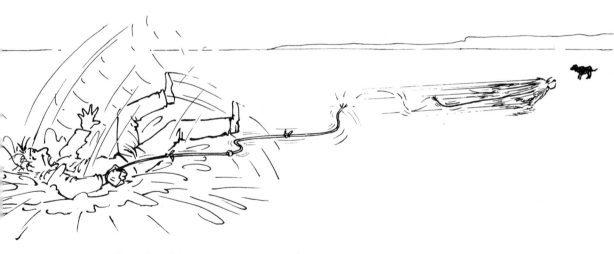

Over Confidence (can result in sound thrashing of dog – if you ever catch him)

Walking the Dog (on the rope)

Inexorable Spiral (can result in starvation of both parties)

Arrant Lunacy (can result in justified fatality)

Walking the Dog (on a running lead)

Technology has to some extent aided the loony dog-owner through the invention of the spring-loaded 'running lead'.

This device has a handle at the top and a body containing a reel of extending lead which clips to the collar in the usual way. Better models have a control switch which locks the lead in whatever position is desired or leaves it free to unwind or rewind with the dog's perambulations.

Of course, manufacturers will say that for the strongest dog the medium model with a few yards of plastic washing line will suffice. They clearly know little of the power of the loony dog. Get the heavy duty webbing model for use in training ponies.

Whilst no panacea, this invention does at least prevent the lead from dragging on the ground and tripping up all and sundry.

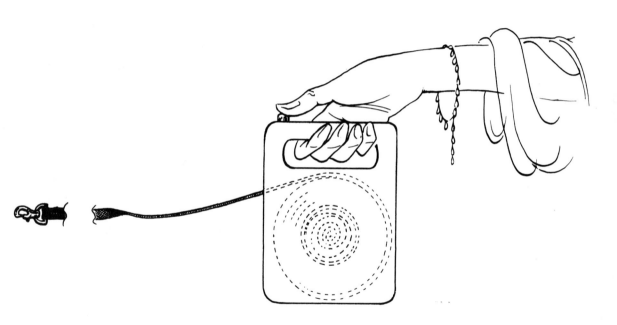

Walking the Dog (on a running lead)

However, a gap exists in the loony dog-owner market for the running lead with super-high-power industrial return spring. This would indeed be a boon and a breakthrough.

Walking the Dog (ad nauseam)

Having discussed the problem of exercise in some depth, the loony dog-owner may reasonably be expected to reach an eventual conclusion concerning the ratio between muscular development and exercise: i.e. The More Exercise A Dog Gets, The Stronger Its Muscles Will Get And The More Exercise It Will Need. The converse also applies.

Many loony dog-owners use this formula to substantiate the total exclusion of 'walkies' from their own and their dog's lives.

The ingenious handyman might even manage an alternative indoor means of exercise on the same principle as the exercise bicycle (*and* save on electricity).

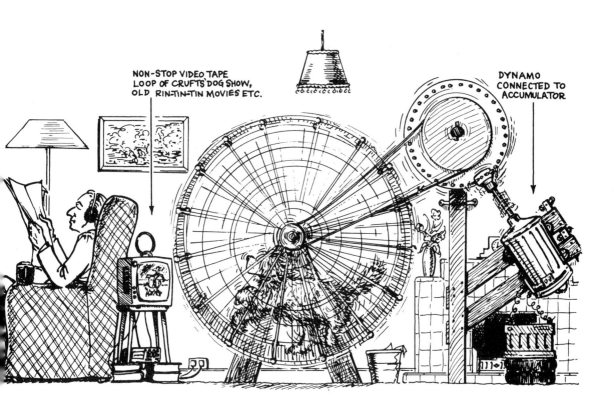

NON-STOP VIDEO TAPE
LOOP OF CRUFTS DOG SHOW,
OLD RIN-TIN-TIN MOVIES ETC.

DYNAMO
CONNECTED TO
ACCUMULATOR

Reward/Punishment

Always give words of encouragement, reward, praise lavishly, pay homage to, genuflect at the paws of, indulge in self-immolation of a fairly gruesome nature as an indelible mark of tribute to the dog who does something right in preference to the dog who does something wrong.

The loony dog-owner should, in the first regard, go out of his way in the rare event of the animal doing something right, to give bounteous rewards, and even do so when he feels a hint that the dog might have fleetingly thought of doing something right even if, in the event, he did it all wrong as usual.

Carried to its logical extreme the constant giving of spurious rewards can result in a much more manageable animal.★

★ Note however that this practice can have unpleasantly disruptive consequences (see 'Toiletting' and 'Methane Output').

Punishment: Striking the Animal

Many experts give strong guidance on this point, which we gladly pass on.

In circumstances of *extreme* provocation the loony dog-owner should be most careful, when inflicting punishment, of causing excessive pain, particularly by the jarring of the bones and tendons of the hand and arm. Bruising and swelling has frequently been suffered by owners following chastisement of the animal.

The loony dog, however, seems to be constructed of a sort of hard resilient rubber which no amount of battering seems to affect. Be warned that a blow to the mutt often means a pain in the arm.

The Urge to Kill

All loony dog-owners will have experience of this and – as a most regrettable raw animal instinct – it should be curbed. It is most commonly experienced during:

(a) Continuous threatening to worry sheep.
(b) Continuous threatening to fight/copulate with other dogs.
(c) Continuous threatening to copulate with sheep (difficult one, this).
(d) Continuous threatening to play with/attack anything that moves which might be a dog. (We have already mentioned some examples of these instinctual canine triggers. Here are some of the more exotic varieties):

Dogs on Wheels

The Urge to Kill

Applicable to Dogs With Poor Eyesight

Very Large Dog

Invisible Dog

The stress caused by these triggers can, of course, be compounded by the high-pitched shrieks which often accompany convulsive over-excitement and frustration.

(e) Any other canine behaviour which turns you into a murderous wreck.

Feeding

His Master's Nosh

Retaliation

How Much to Feed

Calculating the amount to feed the dog is an exacerbated problem for the loony dog-owner.

1. Drag your old bathroom scales on to a reasonably flat surface; 2. Get on to them yourself; 3. Write down weight (this can be a depressing process); 4. Try to catch the dog; 5. Try to pick up the dog and carry him back to the scales from the distant corner of the garden where you managed to corner him; 6. Get on scales and try to look over dog's body at reading without over-balancing as he struggles in your arms; 7. Pick yourself up and write down weight; 8. Now comes the difficult bit; 9. Subtract weight (a) from weight (b) and from the result calculate the dog's daily food requirement remembering the ratio: two-thirds of an ounce of food per pound of the dog's body weight; 10. Two hours and five broken pencils later, discover that cans of dog food are marked in metric weights.

What to Feed

Always remember that the ancestors of your little poochie-poos were slavering great wolves whose first instinct in the wild was to eat the paunch of their victims. This is because the stomach of their prey contained half-digested vegetable matter which supplemented their meat diet.

This gratuitously disgusting piece of information says more about the demeanour of the loony dog than about its diet. However, most dogs will eat virtually anything you give them (except some namby-pamby pedigree breeds) including foul-smelling tripe, rubbish, lights, light-shades, melts, old shoes, liver, bacon, tomatoes, fried onion-rings and french fries, new shoes, umbrella stands, hearts, flowers, kidneys, fireside rugs and your wallet if you leave it around. Ridiculously expensive canned food is little better and it is interesting to compare the odour given off by a freshly-opened can and that produced at some time after feeding from the dog's rear end. (Are we twigging something here?) (see 'Methane Output')

Toiletting*

Having looked at feeding, we move to the other end (so to speak) of the spectrum. The loony dog will often sleep in the kitchen or a similar room, where quarry tiles are ideal, and some of the modern vinyl floor coverings are acceptable (but watch for seepage under the lino when an accident occurs near a wall – it can take months to discover where the smell is coming from). After removal of solids with a shovel and garden trowel – or suitable implement – use a proprietary brand of cleaner and finally mop over with dilute disinfectant. This so annoys the loony dog that he will probably want to re-'mark' the spot the next night.

* This fairly repellent subject has to be faced but will be dealt with in as little space as possible.

What To Do With Waste Products

On rare occasions evacuation of the bowels and bladder can be achieved outside the happy home. Various techniques are involved.

If the loony dog-owner keeps a careful mental note of the last time the bowels were opened it should be possible to predict the approximate time of the subsequent movement, taking into account times and types of feed, exercise, etc. However, the animal seems to have an instinctual response to this approach and can sometimes hold himself in for days or squat two or three times a day at will.

Considering that the loony dog-owner is performing a laudable social service (albeit through necessity) by refraining from adding to the vast quantities of canine faecal matter which cover our streets and public places, it is a bitter irony that his only reward is the problem of disposal of the waste products which build up in the garden.

Burying is one solution but you will soon run out of places in which to dig holes. If a full-time hobby is required why not invest in a chemical toilet for the dog? Well, plenty of reasons why not, actually, but certainly this prolific effluvium will accumulate in a few short weeks.

Imaginative means of disposal are outside the brief of the present volume and it must be left to the ingenuity – not to say desperation of the readers . . .*

* Cop-out.

NO GO AREA

Vets and Drugs and Bark and Growl

Terminal Halitosis

Vets and Drugs and Bark and Growl

Methane Output

Vets and Drugs and Bark and Growl

Methane Output. Only too common, the bout of fiery flatulence is often due to dietary idiosyncrasies.

Next time, make sure you put the kitchen bin out of the dog's reach (*and* the vegetable rack), keep him away from the compost heap, make sure all the cupboards containing food (or substances such as flour and washing powder which can be spread around the floor) are padlocked and put the fruit bowl on top of the bookcase.

Vets and Drugs and Bark and Growl

The loony dog-owner will soon discover that his animal is as tough as a battalion's worth of old corps boots in terms of physical condition, but occasionally the veterinary surgeon has to be consulted (for necessary jabs, etc.).

The actual details of any medical complaints needn't concern us here but various tactical manoeuvres involved in the visit are important to avoid the bedlam resulting from sitting with the loony dog in the waiting room surrounded by other disturbed and disturbing pets.

The participation of two lucky volunteers is essential.

Phase 1   **Phase 2**

Vets and Drugs and Bark and Growl

Phase 3: Zero Hour   **Phase 4: Running the Gauntlet**

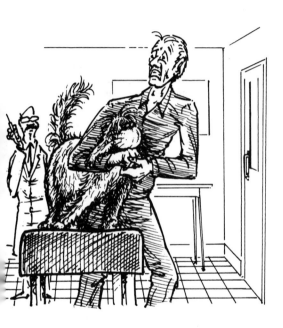

Phase 5: The Examination Table Headlock

Phase 6: Rapid Escape Leaving Assistant to Pay Over-blown Bill.

Vets and Drugs and Bark and Growl

Basically, the vet can do very little to treat the convulsive behaviour of the true loony dog (short of homeopathic hypnotherapy with acupuncture) but it might be worth trying pills such as muscle relaxants, pills which alter the balance of chemicals in the brain (e.g. Mogadog), veterinary deodorant pills (for bad breath and wind), tranquillizers (for the loony dog-owner) etc.

As the instinct of the animal goes into over-drive at the sight of anything dog-like, noticeable benefits are often illusory, but like the drowning man clutching at straws you may find yourself administering up to eight tablets a day for the rest of the dog's life in the hope of behaviour modification.

Administering pills can also be a problem. . . .

Lacing the Food

Vets and Drugs and Bark and Growl

The Alternate Tablet/Choc Drop Ploy

The Lion's Mouth

Stud Purposes

Careful readers will have realised that *The Loony Dog-owner's Handbook* concerns itself purely with the male of the species. Bitches, it would appear, have certain unpleasant and messy habits concerning 'seasons' and scent glands and so forth and therefore can have no place, apart from the incidental, in the present volume. However, the 'cock' animal presents a somewhat more straightforward problem.

Most dog owners do everything in their power to prevent the increase of the dog population (see also 'Castration', 'Spaying', 'Re-Spaying', '1000-Mile Service', 'Buckets of Cold Water', 'Methods of Contraception and Why They Won't Work'). A small number of owners are unlucky enough to possess pedigree breeds and some of these poor fools are misguided enough to want to encourage their dogs to breed. (See 'Filthy Lucre'.)

In the remote event of the loony dog-owner actually wishing to propagate the species and inflict the progeny upon unsuspecting mankind (and vice versa), we urge the following advice. Extract the largest possible cash remuneration from the bitch-owner, by frequently reiterating your willingness to waive your right to the first of the litter.

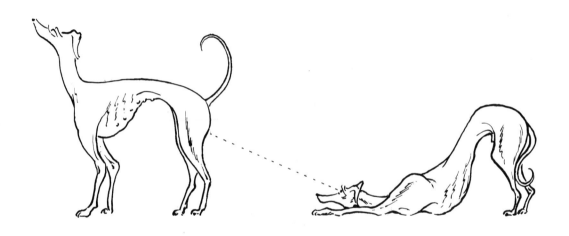

Natural Instincts Such as Mating Have Been Blunted In Many Pedigrees By Selective Breeding.

Stud Purposes

Many Mongrels, However, Have No Trouble in Managing the Foreplay Stage . . .

. . . Yet Their Genetic Memory Can Still Fail Them.

Stud Purposes

Which bits go where is a matter of trial and error (see 'Annoying the Visitors'). Suffice to say that the correct linkage is often achieved in the street and up back alleys, so to speak, (witness the number of the little blighters around the place) and the process can drag on for hours under controlled conditions.

To Avoid Embarrassment For the Delicate Reader, Wooden Dolls Have Been Used
To Represent the Dogs in This Illustration.

An unusual physiological feature is the inability of the dogs to disengage 'during'. Sometimes the poor copulating bitch needs to give her back a rest and the animals rearrange as follows:

Book Ends

If achieved, this gives everybody a good laugh during the inordinately long performance and makes extrication particularly tricky.

Grooming

Brushing Vigorously in the Direction of the Fur

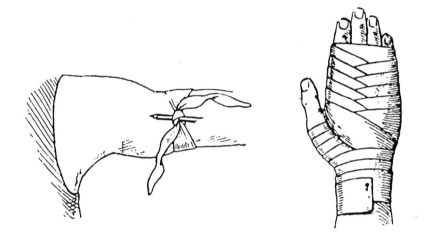

Applying a Tourniquet

Travel in the Car

To avoid walking the dog on the public highways and byways, the loony dog-owner will inevitably resort to vehicular means of transport to the most desertedly dog-free spot for exercise purposes.

If the dog (*and* you) last that long, the chances are that you will eventually run through a number of different vehicles in an attempt to suit the proclivities of the dog.

Car 1: The Saloon (total havoc)

Car 2: The Estate With Dog Guard (contained havoc)

The next option is to give the rear side-windows of Car 2 a coat of white emulsion on the inside to obstruct the loony dog's view of instinctual triggers outside the car. (Never forget the sharpness of canine hearing.) One nihilistic diversion is to leave the dog in the parked vehicle and watch the creation of your own abstract work of art on the rear window as a dog passes and the car rocks from side to side★. Here is a fine example of the form.

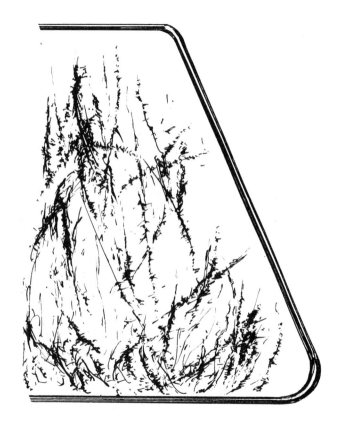

★ Extra pleasure can be gained from the painstaking removal of showers of dandruff-like paint flakes from the interior of the car.

Car 3: The Hatchback With Rear Shelf Removed and Home-made Frame With Grille Inserted

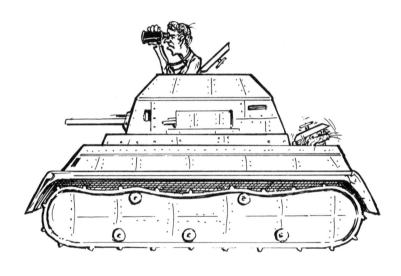

Car 4: The Ideal Vehicle For Travel With the Loony Dog

Coping With Other Dog Lovers

Carefully study the situation on the page opposite and answer the following:

This woman has cornered you in a public park. What do you say?
1. Laugh in a hysterically light-hearted manner and say, 'I'm afraid he's a bit over-excitable.'
2. 'How do you keep your dog's lead so shiny?'
3. 'Go on then, madam, call the R.S.P.C.A.'
4. 'My dog is a psychopath and I am the only thing standing between your little Fido and total annihilation.'
5. 'If your concern is genuine, please accept this animal as a gift.'
6. 'How dare you interrupt our training for Crufts!'
7. 'As he's nearly pulling my arm out of its socket I don't *care* if I'm hurting his throat.'
8. 'Weather's not bad for the time of year, eh?'
9. 'Personally I prefer butcher's meat to this tinned rubbish, don't you?'

Advertiser's Announcements

MEN-o-PAWS

SIGNET RING

For the broody bitch in **your** life...this life-like human hand (with or without handsome signet ring) will give her something to gnaw at during those hot flushes.
£7.50 each (Code: MoP)
£13.00 pair (Code: MoPair) — state male or female
(Realistic red vegetable dye — 50p extra).

BLINKEROO

Cut down the likelihood of your canine companion's distraction during walks by limiting his field of vision with these very becoming accoutrements. Finished in artificial fleece-lined antelope. *With bridle £5.00 the pair or £3.50 (for singles for dogs blind in one eye — state right or left). (Code: BOO).*

DOWNBOYDOWN

Recapture the beautiful memories of your departed pet when he's gone to that great kennel in the sky. This fine headstone hand-crafted in moulded plexi-marble (6' high × 2' wide) with realistic paw-print and choice of names. Will grace any flowerbed or patio. *£29.58 each (Code: DBD).*

DOGGY DIAPER

Stop further embarrassment! No more need to house-train! Safe, hygienic and disposable! Each diaper in a choice of cheerful colours is stretchy and superabsorbent! Needs changing only every three weeks of normal diet! (Note handy aperture for tail).
(Also provides a source of entertainment when dog cocks leg and nothing happens.)
£7.50 (pack of 3). (Code: DD).

Fed up with putting your foot in it? Your worries are over: when trade-marks are left on the lawn just pop over a Patent Poochie Poopa Protecta. Finished in attractive terra cotta-type plastic, it will prevent mucky shoes and carpets (and **you** slipping over and landing yourself right in it!) As the weeks go by you can build up quite an array, suitable as stands for attractive pot plants — always a good talking-point with visitors.
£1.50 each (Code: P-P-P-P).

Patent Poochie Poopa Protecta

DIDDY DOGGY BOBBY SOCKS

Help Fido keep his soft pads warm and prevent muddy paw-marks, scratched furniture and human flesh with our latest product in high quality imitation sack-cloth. *1 pair – £3.00; 3 pairs – £7.00 (available in 7 shades of brown – state which).*

DOG BED

For the ultimate in luxury for your adored companion this superb regency-style four poster takes the biscuit. Takes only 2 hours to erect, measures 3′ × 6′ × 5′ and is ideal for use with our Heavy Petty Pamper Pillow *(Code: H.P.P.P.),* Super Snuggle Doggie Duvet *(Code: S.S.D.D.),* Interior Sprung Mutt's Mattress *(Code: I.S.M.M.)* and Poodle Puddle Preventor Rubber Sheet for Rover *(Code: P.P.P.R.S.R.).* Also converts into an imposing sarcophagus for the afterlife of Fido. *(Code D.B.). Complete set: £8,750.28*

FREE!! With every order over £250.00!! We will send you a free DOG*!!. To make use of all that new equipment!! Subject to availability, mongrels only. (*Bitch, slightly pregnant).

Copyright © Borin Van Loon 1985

All rights reserved

First published in Great Britain in 1985
by Century Publishing Co. Ltd,
Portland House, 12–13 Greek Street,
London W1V 5LE

ISBN 0 7126 0764 1

Typeset by Phoenix Photosetting, Chatham
Printed in Great Britain in 1985
by Richard Clay (The Chaucer Press) Ltd,
Bungay, Suffolk

PORTRAIT OF THE
AUTHOR AS A YOUNG
DOG